CW01665475

Círculo Rojo

2018 to 2023
The best moment to buy or invest on a property in Spain

2018 to 2023
The best moment to buy or invest on a property in Spain

Read this book before buying your house or investing on the real estate market in Spain, it will surely help you take the best decision.

Adrián Barbudo

Círculo Rojo
EDITORIAL

Primera edición: febrero 2018

ISBN: 978-84-9183-779-4
Impresión y encuadernación: Editorial Círculo Rojo

Editorial Círculo Rojo

www.editorialcirculorojo.com

info@editorialcirculorojo.com

Impreso en España - Printed in Spain

Acknowledgments

First of all to my family, my wife Maite, who always supports me unconditionally in any project I want to start, especially in the most ambitious one: build our family together.

To my daughters, Paula and Adriana, my greatest treasure. It is a real pleasure to see how they grow up, how they wake up everyday and share my life with them.

To my mother, a reliable person who never lets me down. To my brother for his compliments, but particularly for his criticism.

To my father, an example to follow as for his spirit of improvement, his persistence … among many other qualities, a fighter who never gives up.

To each client and professional I had the opportunity to spend my time with, a well spent time in which I always learnt something.

And to Noelia González Valero for her good and wise advice for the wording of this book and for her translation.

INDEX

Prologue

"Don't let anybody come to you without leaving better and happier" (Mother Teresa of Calcutta)

What you hold on your hands reflects, in my humble opinion, one of the most famous statements in the recent history of mankind: reading a good book always makes a difference for the reader, and if it is about something as important as purchasing a property, under the premise of building a family home and being happy, even more.

The decision to purchase a property is probably one of the most important decisions in our life, since we often compromise our happiness and our family's happiness in that decision, what is very significant for most of us and also for the author.

Most of us either have already purchased a property or are about to purchase one or intend to do it in the future and perhaps, in that moment, we would have wished to have a trustworthy professional near us who helped us in such an important decision, wouldn't we?

In the book you hold on your hands, you will find information about the real estate market in Spain, as well as data, statistics and suggestions which I am sure you will find very useful as guidance and assistance for purchasing a property led by an expert professional in this industry such as Adrián Barbudo.

I met Adrián some months ago in Alicante in one of my conferences about the keys to improve attitude in work teams. Once I finished my speech, we enjoyed a breakfast meeting where we exchanged opinions regarding the subject and we immediately connected, since there was something which united us from the beginning: people and, specifically, our commitment and wish to help others by means of our profession and, in his case, by means of training sales teams or writing a book about the subject he better knows and controls: the real estate market in Spain.

Behind the author of this book, there is a self-made person who best enjoys spending a Sunday at home with his family, cooking together, drawing with his two daughters, watching a film and eating popcorn…etc. In brief, a humble and simple life around his home and family.

Professionally, what I would better highlight of Adrián after getting to know him in depth is his capacity to listen, empathize and be thoughtful: he pays attention to small or big details which may please others and which make the difference. Additionally, I would also highlight his constancy and commitment which undoubtedly helped him to write this book, as well as his sincerity, which I could note from the first minute when he offered me the possibility to write the prologue of his book, what I greatly thank him.

For me, it is not surprising that all these skills make him perfectly understand clients, put him on their shoes and therefore be the leading guide who everybody would wish to have in order to make the always hard decision of purchasing a property.

Client's understanding just involves understanding their 'map', which will allow us to find out what 'value' is for him/her. Our author listens to, empathizes with and puts him on the client's shoes, and finally he suggests alternatives which help the client to make the best decision. For him, it is the key to success. Thus, we can awake sensory acuity aimed to connect with the other person to generate a relational synergy, an essential aspect in every client relationship, as well as personal relationships.

This is the capacity of mirror neurons, these neurons get activated by means of observing an activity, in the same way as when we do it. They allow us feel happiness or sadness when watching a film, as well as when listening to somebody's story, as if it was happening to us. These neurons are associated to imitation and empathy processes which raise sensory acuity making us understand our interlocutor and Adrián showed me he is an excellent expert in that Thus, I recommend him.

What you hold on your hands is the result of many years of experience, hours of work and improvement: a guidebook which aims to train and help you make the decision of purchasing a property in Spain where your dreams will start to come true. Enjoy it!

Javier Giménez Divieso

Senior Executive | Executive and Team Coach | PNL | Trainer | Mentor | Conference speaker

MEETING THE AUTHOR:

I was born in Segovia, a small city full of history which is close to Madrid, in July 1981. Nowadays, I live in Alicante with my wife and my two daughters.

I studied in the University Domingo de Soto (ascribed to the Madrid Complutense University) where I was awarded with the Degree in Business Administration and Management.

I have been working in the real estate market for over 13 years. I feel really passionate about this market so I studied at the University Camilo Jose Cela to become a Real Estate Agent and then I finished my Master's Degree in City Planning and Real Estate Management.

In 2017 I co-funded Koury, an e-commerce corporation in the United States.

I am a hopelessly optimist who is always positive and enthusiastic.

Always learning!!

Some opinions of clients and professionals from my Linkedin profile:

'Adrian Barbudo is one of the best real-estate agents I have met in my 20 years as entrepreneur in this business. He is most devoted and professional in all means and delivers service almost 24/7. In addition he is a very kind, trustworthy and polite person that goes along with everybody. I am 100% satisfied with the job he has done with sales of my plots and houses in Spain and I can recommend him to any customer'

Client

'I have bought two apartments in Spain during the last three years with the assistance of Adrian. His language skills are good and he is always friendly and professional. You'll always get a quick response from him, and he was very helpful to me when it came to dealing with all the bureaucracy related to owning a property in Spain. If you're looking to purchase a property in Spain, I would recommend you to contact Adrian'

Client

'Adrián is a skilled, expeditious, efficient and kind professional with his work. He speaks several languages and is proficient at problem-solving, at work and at mediating among the parties thanks to his optimal aptitudes to get the targets aimed in any job, business or investment'

Notary Public

'Looking for an apartment in Spain Costa Blanca, Adrian's assistance was instrumental in finding the right apartment as well as settling the deal with the seller/developer. I recommend Adrian as efficient and trustworthy. His service went well beyond what a realtor is expected to do'

Client

'I have worked with Adrian for several years, Adrian is always happy to provide information about the latest product releases and pass on his vast area knowledge, his communication skills are excellent, he has patience, and is always willing to go the extra mile with colleagues and customers. He is very talented, sales focused, driven, hard-working, warm co-worker and a joy to work with!'

Costa Activa Estate Agency

'Adrián Barbudo is the perfect example of what happens when two worlds connect. An exemplary professional, Adrián is the type of person you hope you'll meet when visiting a foreign country. He is straight up, knowledgeable about his field and will go the extra mile to meet a client's needs. I was so impressed meeting someone so dedicated and hope I have the opportunity to use his expertise again in the near future. If anyone is looking to buy Property in Spain, please connect with Adrián Barbudo'

Client

'Adrián is a great professional with an extensive experience and expertise in the real estate market, both about the market in general and about the banking system in particular. He deals properly with clients, negotiations and the closing of operations. He is very hard-working and easy-going'.

-Business Manager of the
Eastern Regional Division, Anida (BBVA)

'Adrián is a reliable and efficient professional. It is really easy to work with him and he optimizes time in an excellent way. He is young, trained and with a great experience in the market as well as with expertise in the characteristics thereof. He is clear, direct and transparent'

Business Manager at Sabadell Bank

'I have dealt with Adrian over the past 10 months and I would have to say, as an estate agent he went over and above his duty to me while I concluded a property deal in San Juan Alicante. Adrian consistently made himself available for my questions and throughout this time never failed to assist me as an overseas buyer in the Alicante property market. I would have no hesitation in recommending Adrian to anyone, Spanish or overseas who is considering looking for an agent to assist to find the correct property in the greater Alicante area'

Client

'Adrian is a very capable real estate liaison. Can express himself in good English and is always willing to help his customers out, be it with advice or supporting them with connecting them to the right people in Spain. You may rest assured when you buy through him you get a full service'

Client

‘Adrian is an excellent property consultant. He has extensive knowledge and understanding of the Spanish real estate market’

Client

Presentation

By writing this book, I am embarking on a new project which has been in my mind for years. I have waited until I finished my Master's Degree in Urban Planning and Real Estate Management to devote my time to the thrilling adventure which is writing a book. As in other prior experiences, I mainly seek to get personal satisfaction and learn –once I read that the best way to become an expert or having a great expertise in an area is writing a book because it forces you to do a research which, otherwise, you will never do, and I agree with this idea.

Personally, I have been doing a specific research and learning for a long time to be able to write this book and, certainly, it is not an easy work at all.

However, when you love what you do to earn a living, it is never considered work.

This easy-to-read book is addressed to any person or corporation which is considering investing on the real estate market, but which still has not made the decision to go forward or go ahead with this idea for any reason.

It is not surprising the fact that it is a hard decision which may sometimes delay for months or even years. Actually, a family purchasing a property is not just purchasing the square meters that worry so much to some clients, the width of the living room or the modernity of the kitchen, but they are also making the decision whether that place is appropriate to build a home, to wake up everyday, to rest, to enjoy with friends...

Many of my clients purchase properties thinking of their near future, understanding that they will need more space when the moment to build a family comes.

Let's think that over the 80% of people will only purchase a house in their lives and the 78% of the purchases of houses are funded with a loan which, as we will see later, last 23 years and 4 months as an average.

The 12% of Spanish people have two properties, the 3% have three and the 1% has more than three. These data help us realize how important is the decision to purchase a house.

And, what does worry all of us? Knowing whether we will be able to meet the mortgage payments for so many years, as the recent history shown us that such payments cannot be sometimes met and we end up losing the property in favour of the banking institutions.

Therefore, it is understandable that the decision to purchase something which requires so many payment years needs to be discussed and agreed by the different members of a family as well as the fact that making this decision may be frightening and stressful because it is probably one of the most important or crucial decisions which you will make in your life. Perhaps, it just goes after deciding when is the best moment to build a family -you will never find a good moment to build family, you just have to dare and do it, and like when you purchase your house, they are wonderful moments.

How many times I failed to sell a property because the couple did not agree whether it was the best moment or not to purchase that property, or whether the price was a bit high for their budget, or whether the mortgage share was a bit excessive and it went beyond their initial calculations, making them not be sure whether they could make ends meet! The decision may turn hard and complicated and for that reason it is easy that a purchaser "cools down".

So, in order to help make such a complicated decision, I tried to make clear the current situation by combining historical indicators, which allow measurement and monitoring, with my own opinions generated by the interpretation of figures and my own experience selling properties for more than 13 years.

I tried to support the figures with graphs so as to make it easier understand and interpret them. A simple glance to a graph will be enough to understand the moment which the real estate market is experiencing in Spain and why **now** is a good moment to purchase your house.

During the last years, we have been living surrounded by the word crisis and, undoubtedly, one of the most affected businesses or markets is the real estate.

However, now we know, according to the data, that it is a good moment to **PURCHASE OR INVEST ON REAL ESTATE IN SPAIN** and we can also take advantage of a really cheap funding trend, which is expected to continue for the short time.

An old friend told me once: Adrián, you have to purchase when the investment asset (real estate, stock…) is on the rise, that is, do not try to guess whether the product has bottomed out and it is at its lowest level or whether its price will go on decreasing, just wait until it raises for a continuous period to be sure of its upward trend. It is true that with this idea you will obviously not 'enter' into the investment the first one, but at the same time it is a policy to try to avoid unpleasant surprises and try to ensure a bit more the profitability and the invested money.

If you are close to retirement and you are reading this book, think that investing on real estate is a perfect supplement for your pension. Nowadays, it is certainly the best and most reliable alternative in the market.

If you are truly interested in finding out the current situation of the real estate market in Spain to purchase a house, please continue reading and you will surely find interesting the rest of this book. I hope you find this book worthy and, above all, that it encourages you to act.

The final Checklist to buy a property in Spain

The idea of buying a property to build a home to share with your family and friends is really exciting.

From the start, when you search properties on the Internet, arrange visits to find out whether it is or it isn't your dream house, until the end of the purchase process in the Notary's Office when you wear your heart on your sleeve, with a mix of feelings: enthusiasm, excitement, happiness and, above all, anxiety to sleep in your property for the first time.

I still remember perfectly when my wife and I bought our first property. We were two youngsters who had finished university just a couple of years before and who, in fact, did not have life experience. But what we both knew was that we wanted to build a home together, so we decided to go for it.

The phase of searching a property took us some weeks, but we finally found our ideal property. So, once we were sure about what property we wanted to purchase, we had to solve the funding. Thus, we negotiated our mortgage with different banks until we got the best option, the one which was suitable for us in that moment because of the interest rate, the mortgage term... Without realizing, we were in the Notary's Office: Robert (the seller), us, our family acting as guarantors, the Manager of the bank and the Notary. The atmosphere was filled with happiness and positive energy. Few hours after finishing in the Notary's Office, we were having dinner with our family for the first time in our new property, which was becoming our home, full of life and happiness, to which few years later will join our daughters, Paula and Adriana.

Purchasing YOUR PROPERTY is one of the most important moments in your life and the most expensive acquisition you will ever make. Therefore, do not purchase before hiring a REAL ESTATE AGENT, who will always watch over your interests as a purchaser, controlling the purchase process at any moment, and who will be BY YOUR SIDE and will help you negotiate to get your most important requirements and demands.

Now, read carefully the Checklist (which slightly varies whether you purchase a new construction or a second-hand property) so that your purchase is safer and you avoid unpleasant surprises.

New construction property:

1- Verify the submission and record of the WORK COMPLETION CERTIFICATE, the document which certifies that the works finished and all the necessary licenses according to law have been granted.

2- Check that the property is free of encumbrances by means of a NON-CERTIFIED EXTRACT, which is probably the most important document. The non-certified extract provides the updated recorded information of the property, as well as its description.

3- First Occupancy License issued by the City Council of the city where the property is located. A very important document which expires in 10 years. Should you have to renew it or request a Second Occupancy License, you have to hire the services of an architect.

4- Descriptive and graphic Cadastral Certificate. This document is gotten in the Cadastral Registry, which is the Real Estate Statistics Authority in a city. It includes a physical, financial and legal description of rural and urban properties.

5- Water installation report, necessary to hire water supply.

6- Electricity installation report, necessary to hire electricity supply (sometimes, the electricity installation report is not compulsory and the First Occupancy License would be enough to hire the electricity supply).

7- Gas installation report, necessary to hire gas supply.

8- A certificate of the Owners' Community which states the debt situation.

9- Real Estate Tax. Check whether there are outstanding payments for this tax.

10- Community By-laws, so you can know the regulations governing the residential development.

11- The Energy Performance Certificate. This document shows the energy performance of the property. In addition, it is compulsory to have this document for the property rental. It expires in 10 years.

12- The payment receipts made on account up to the date when the Title Deed is signed, together with a receipt of the last payment made (whether it is a bank transfer or a bank cheque).

Second-hand property:

1- Non-certified extract. Check the current situation of the property, as well as the fact that the seller is its owner and that the property is free of charges and encumbrances.

2- Request the Second Occupancy License whether the First Occupancy License has expired. This document will be necessary to hire water, electricity and gas supply.

3- A descriptive and graphic Cadastral Certificate. This document is gotten in the Cadastral Registry, which is the Real Estate Statistics Authority in a city. It includes a physical, financial and legal description of rural and urban properties.

4- The last bills of the different supplies such as electricity, gas and water. Check that there are no outstanding payments. Pay attention to this point: No Notary checks the existence of debts regarding these supplies and sometimes these debts may be high.

5- A certificate of the Owners' Community which states the debt situation.

6- Ask for the last Real Estate Tax receipt and check that there are no debts from prior years.

7- The Energy Performance Certificate. This document shows the energy performance of the property. In addition, it is compulsory to have this document for the property rental. It expires in 10 years.

8- The payment receipts made on account up to the date when the Title Deed is signed, together with a receipt of the last payment made (whether it is a bank transfer or a bank cheque).

9- Whether the purchased property was subject to a mortgage, you have to request to the bank a certificate of the outstanding debt on the day of the Title Deed's signature. Regardless the existence of a monetary debt, if the mortgage still appears in the Registry, then an amount must be withheld to the seller for the Registry's cancellation of the mortgage. Pay attention to this provision: you cannot forget it, since it sometimes amounts to around 1,000€.

In addition, in your case, foreigner reader, you must apply for a N.I.E., which is the Foreigner Identification Number. You have to apply for this document in the National Police Station by means of a prior arrangement. You will need a passport photograph, a passport copy, your original passport and two fulfilled forms. You can carry out this process in the Spanish Embassy or Consulate of any country across the world, in order to make it easy. This document is utterly important, since you cannot record as a public deed any property, purchase a car or open a bank account without it.

Why is it a good moment to invest in Spain now?

In this chapter I will try to show you the situation of the real estate market in the past, the present and where it goes in the future in Spain.

Observing the figure 1, which shows a graph from the Spanish National Statistics Institute (INE), we can see that the trend of the amount of purchase-sale operations, in the percentage of housing price variation, keeps an upward line, breaking the downward trend for the first time in the 4th quarter of 2011, which will be repeated until the 4th quarter of 2012. From that date, the housing price has been increasing, considering that quarter as the one with the lowest data of all of them, with a -12.8 variation.

Nowadays, we can appreciate an upward trend and the housing price is increasing at a rate over the **+5% a year**.

However, the data shown in this graph are at a domestic level, what implies an average throughout all the country, but we must become aware that the real estate market performs differently depending on the area we take into account. For that reason, a city such as Avila has not had the same correction of prices or purchase-sale levels that a city such as Alicante, as well as the rate at which the market increases in a city such as Zamora is different to a city such as Madrid.

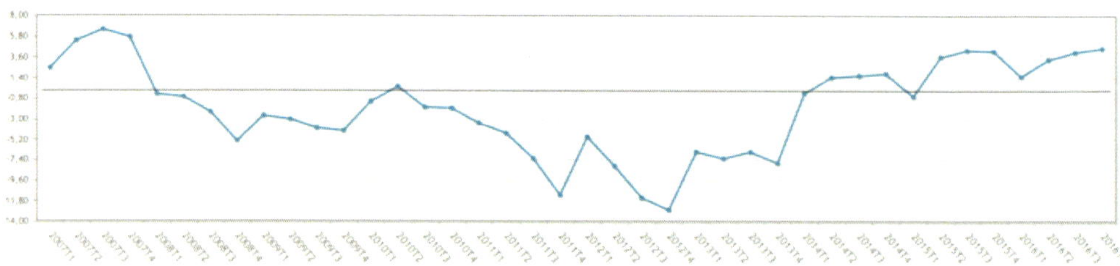

Source: INE (fig 1)

Housing price reached its peak in 2007, as we can see in the graph 2, with a 101.417 rate in the third quarter when a first slight decrease started, getting sharper at the beginning of 2010 and reaching a 63.642 rate in the first quarter of 2014. Such variation from the highest point to the lowest is of 37.77 points.

From that moment, it becomes an upward trend, slow and slight, but apparently reliable.

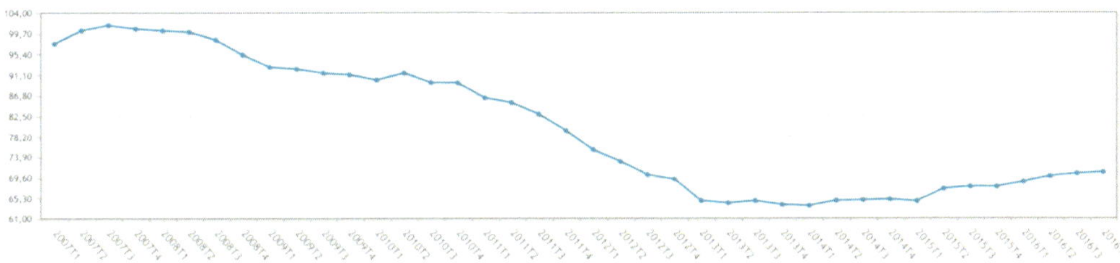

Source: INE (fig 2)

The next graph, figure 3, shows as the housing price stated in Euros per square meter reached its peak in 2007 with a value of 2,048€/m2 (the peak of the housing bubble). From that moment, the price keeps a downward line until reaching the value of 1,202€/m2 in 2014, the lowest price shown in the graph, what implies a 41.01% reduction from peaks and a downward trend which lasted 7 years.

From the year 2014, the price varies its performance and we can observe an increase, which is again slight and apparently firm, until reaching the price of 1,258€/m2 in the year 2017, at the same level than in 2013.

As I said at the beginning of this book, this upward trend comes from a long time, in this case from the year 2015, that is, the price of houses per m2 has increased for the last two years. What does it mean? That it is a wonderful time to purchase.

(fig 3)

The non-residential real estate investment up to the third quarter of 2017 increased a 60% and it suggests that 2017 is going to be a record year.

In the figure 4, we can see that the Funds are the greatest investors, followed by the Real Estate Agencies. It also indicates that the main source of investments comes from Europe.

International funds are still the unquestionable protagonists and the available-for-sale assets are the key in the typology-driven investment on real estate. Most of the banks sold their real estate portfolios to investment funds. BBVA sold its portfolio managed by Anida to Cerberus, an American investment fund, being the last bank to join this trend.

Funds or great investors' interest in Spain is certainly great news and a better sign of the situation we are experiencing.

We are talking about corporations which only value numbers as to profitability, what means that if these corporations are interested in investing in Spain, why is it not going to be interesting for small investors or families?

EVOLUTION OF NON-RESIDENTIAL REAL ESTATE INVESTMENT
In thousands of million Euros

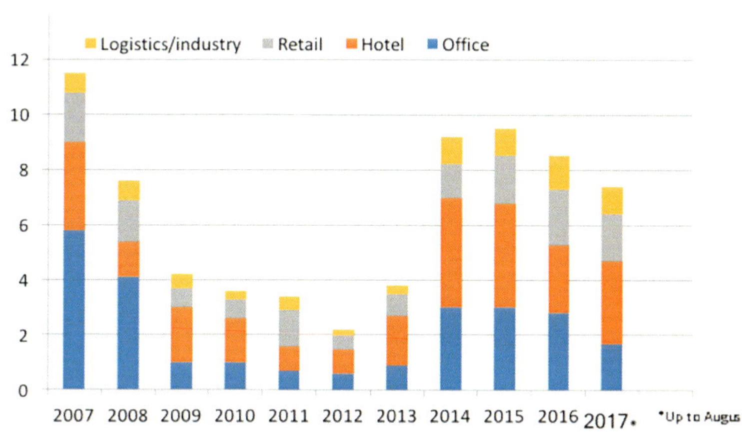

Volume in 2017 In percentage

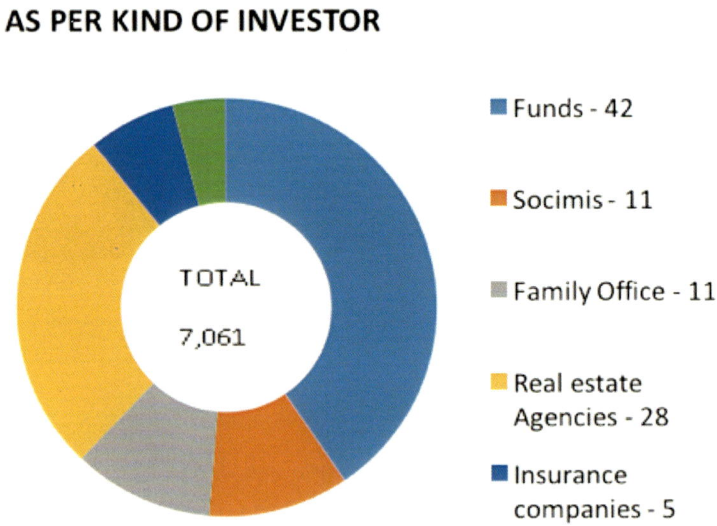

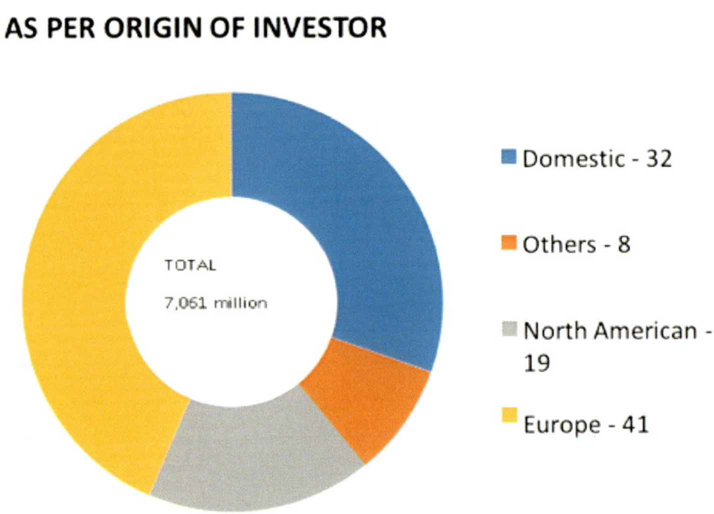

Source: Expansión (fig 4)

Coming back to the purchase-sale housing market, in Madrid the price increased a 15.5% in the last twelve months (from September 2016 to September 2017), with a 2.7% inter-annual increase in the second quarter of the year.

The domestic average of the inter-annual evolution of the average housing value is over the 5%.

Properties in the coast are regulated differently due to the relevance of foreign clients as we will see in another chapter later.

In 2016, there was a 14.6% increase in the purchases and sales in coastal cities, among which we must highlight Torrevieja, Marbella, Orihuela and Mijas. In the same year, Orihuela, Torrevieja, Elche and Benidorm led the granting of new construction certificates followed by Barcelona, Malaga, Almeria and Valencia.

The recovery in the Mediterranean is, in general, ahead of the Atlantic and Cantabrian coasts, as it is shown in the figure number 5.

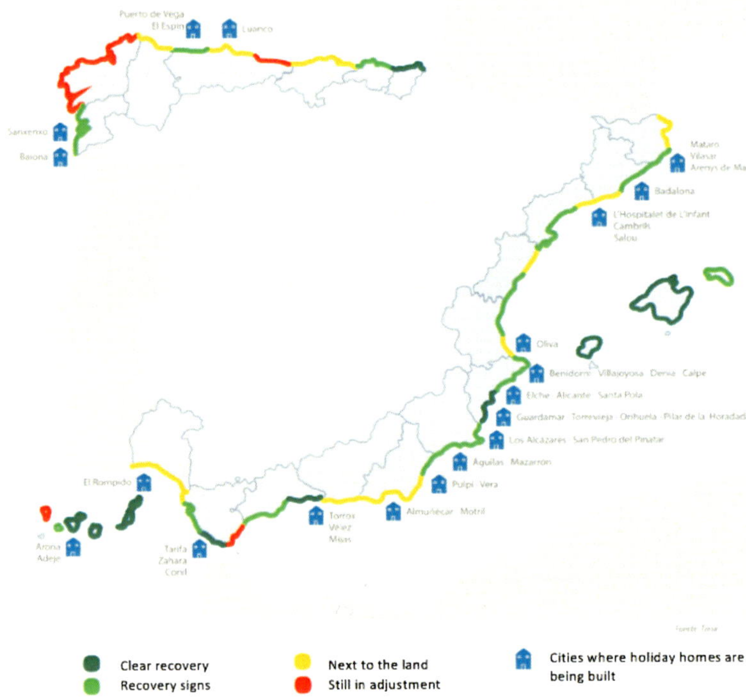

Source: Tinsa (fig 5)

The real estate market is experiencing a moment in which all the indicators show the same trend: an upward trend as to the amount of housing purchase-sale operations, mortgage granting and, above all, the housing price. It is also true that we find some exceptions because there are still areas such as Zamora, Teruel, Soria and Cuenca, for instance, where the second-hand housing prices are still decreasing.

Taking as a reference the second quarter of 2017, the provinces with a higher amount of housing purchase-sale operations recorded during the last twelve months are Madrid (63,037), Barcelona (51,010), Alicante (32,068), Malaga (28,271), Valencia (23,644), Balearic Islands (15,158), Seville (13,423), Murcia (12,274), Las Palmas (10,962) and Tenerife (10,602).

48 provinces had inter-annual increases in housing purchase-sale operations, headed by Tarragona (26.56%), Almeria (25.70%), Barcelona (21.29%), Balearic Islands (21.07%) and Tenerife (19.70%).

And what happens if we analyze all the information that we have shown up to this point?

All the figures and graphs are moving in the same direction and following the same trend. **Housing is again the most profitable and reliable asset in the investment market.**

New construction properties

Undoubtedly, one of the first signs that the market is changing and its trend is going upwards is the appearance of new constructions. There are cities or districts in these cities where, at a bird's-eye view, we could count tens of cranes working on the construction of new houses in this moment.

The new construction performance has been one of the most significant changes in the real estate market so far in 2017. The rate of finished new houses increases a 39% compared to the year 2016. In the first quarter of the year, there were 27% more sales than in the same period of the prior year.

However, the importance of new construction compared to the second-hand market is still weak. The second-hand housing market is almost 5 times higher than the new housing market, although this difference will be reduced in the next years due to the increase of new constructions.

In the second quarter of 2017, the purchases and sales of new construction properties stand out in Madrid (3,976), Barcelona (1,709), Malaga (1,212) and Alicante (1,205).

Prime locations such as the beachfront, where prices are higher, are placed without variations in the first position as follows: La Concha in San Sebastian (9,000€/m2), Portixol in Palma de Majorca (8,000€/m2), the seafront promenade of Ibiza (7,000€/m2), Marbella (6,000€/m2) and Benidorm in Alicante, where we can currently find a new construction property promotion for an average price over 8,000€/m2, an emblematic and singular building under construction which will make the difference and become an example to be followed in the Spanish coasts.

Advantages of purchasing new construction properties

In this chapter we are going to list a set of profitable factors of purchasing a new construction property in Spain.

-**Payment method**: the possibility to make payments on account during the construction is a way to make payments easier and increase savings as these amounts are ensured by bank guarantees.

-**Construction insurance** which benefits the purchaser when he/she decides to purchase a new construction property:

- A ten-year liability against problems affecting foundations, beams, bearing walls or other construction elements within 10 years from the construction acceptance.

- Three-year liability against the construction defects or damages causing a breach of the minimum standards of habitability.

- One-year liability against the defects affecting finishing elements or the completion of works.

- In countries such as France or the United Kingdom, as for the sale of a second-house property, there is a report made by the seller and used as a guarantee of the house condition so the purchaser avoids the unpleasant situation of finding hidden defects or problems in the future. However, in Spain it is not necessary to grant any document like that before any Notary Public, except for the Energy Performance Certificate, what makes the purchaser assume a risk as he/she is not aware of the condition of the electrical wiring or the pipes, to give a couple of examples.

-The possibility to adjust small defects in the property for free.

-Customizing the house finishes and sometimes, whether they are single-family houses, not only the finishes but also its layout, or adding additional areas such as a solarium, a basement …

Foreign clients

International clients had a relevance of the **19.5%** on the total of purchase-sale operations in 2016.

The purchase of houses by foreign clients is still growing with an increase over a 13% a year.

Non-resident clients invest an average of 1,368€/m2 in Spain. Chinese clients are the ones who invest the most money per square meter amounting to 2,625€/m2, followed by the Americans with a 2,372 €/m2, the Russians with a 2,319€/m2, the Swedish with a 2.294€/m2 and the Norwegians with a 2,182€7m2.

In the Valencian Community, the investment average value amounts to 1,282€/m2. The leading clients are British, as in the last years, followed by Belgian and French clients, which are the three most important nationalities in this region. However, we must also take into account Italian clients as they are getting more interested in investing in Spain, particularly in the Costa Blanca.

In an Autonomous Community classification, the Canary Islands is the one with the highest foreign demand as the 34% of all the purchases in that region were carried out by foreign people. It is followed by the Balearic Islands (31.7%), the Valencian Community (26%), Murcia (16%), Andalusia (14%) and Catalonia (13.4%).

The most relevant provinces as for the purchase of houses by foreign people in the first quarter of the year, as we can see in the graph 6, were Tenerife (44.2%), Alicante (41%), Girona (33%), the Balearic Islands (31.7%), Malaga (28.2%) and Las Palmas (24%). It means that in Tenerife and Alicante nearly the half of the purchases are carried out by international clients.

All this reflects the relevant role of foreign clients in the Spanish real estate market, especially in the coast. The region's developers are well aware of that and for that reason most of these corporations allocate specific financial resources and personnel. They even may create an international client department which helps not only on sales, but also to understand the client's preferences as for the types of construction, the finishes, the common areas or the interior decoration of the houses which, depending on his/her nationality, may vary. For instance, if you want to sell a property to a Norwegian, make sure that the mattress is soft, as they like it this way.

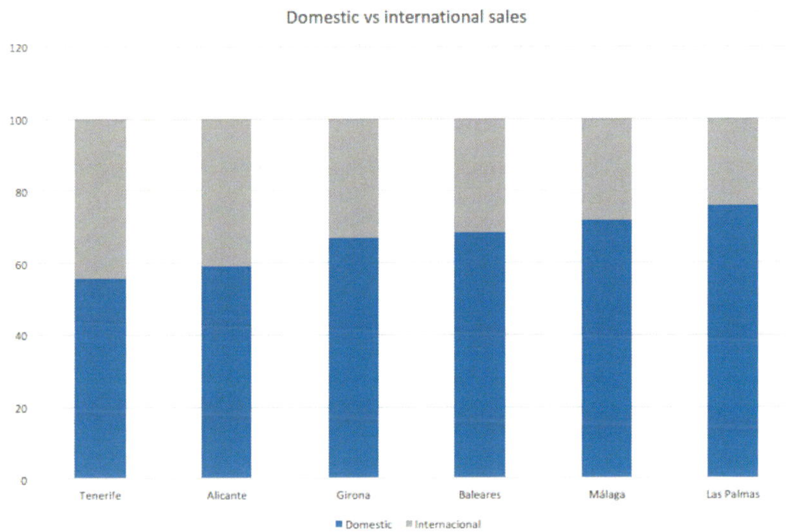

(Fig 6)

The graph in the figure 7, obtained in the Property Registry, shows the property purchase ranking carried out by foreign clients in the second quarter of 2017.

As usual, the leaders of the ranking in Spain are the clients from the United Kingdom, who, despite the voting in favour to exit the European Union carried out on 23rd June 2016, which turned into the so-called Brexit, still do not known how it is going to take place after 16 months. It is true that during the months after the British referendum, the sales of these clients decreased considerably, both due to the uncertainty of the political moment and to the pound depreciation, which dropped up to a 20% for a short period of time. Despite the referendum to abandon the European Union and their currency depreciation, what is clear is the fact that the British are eager to purchase a house in Spain and it is evidenced by the statistics in which they are the leaders of the ranking year after year.

After the United Kingdom, we find France, Germany and in the forth position Belgium, a market which has been taking hold for a couple of years. The Belgian client has an average budget among 200,000 and 250,000€ to purchase a property in Spain.

Property purchases and sales recorded according to the purchaser's nationality 2nd quarter 2017		
Nationalities	**%**	**% foreign people**
United Kingdom	1.95%	14.90%
France	1.11%	8.48%
Germany	1.02%	7.79%
Belgium	0.83%	6.37%
Italy	0.81%	6.17%
Sweden	0.81%	6.17%
Romania	0.70%	5.37%
Morocco	0.56%	4.32%
China	0.53%	4.06%
Russia	0.36%	2.74%
Netherlands	0.33%	2.51%

Norway	0.29%	2.19%
Ukraine	0.23%	1.79%
Algeria	0.20%	1.51%
Poland	0.19%	1.44%
Bulgaria	0.15%	1.17%
Switzerland	0.15%	1.14%
Ireland	0.13%	1.03%
Denmark	0.13%	1.01%
Others	2.60%	19.87%
Foreign people	**13.06%**	**100.00%**

Source: Property Registry (fig 7)

The figure 8 shows the development of the different international markets from 2006 to the 2nd quarter of 2017, reflecting the leadership of British clients.

Development of housing purchases by foreign people per nationality (%)

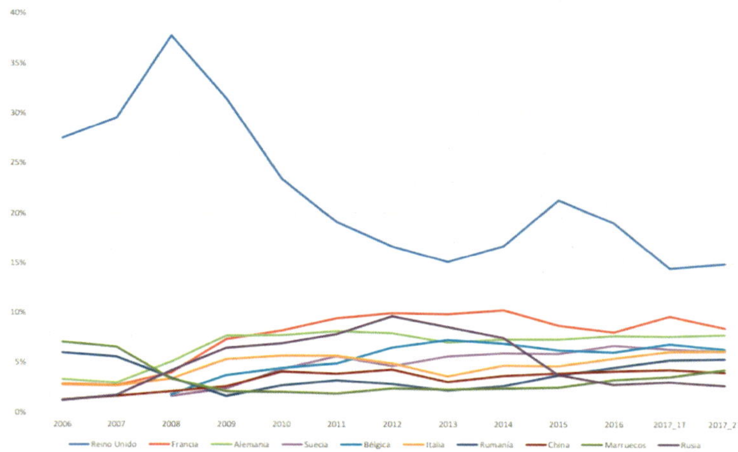

Source: Property Registry (fig 8)

Funding

What is the first thing that comes to my mind if I think of banks? That they started to advertise once again mortgages, personal loans, funding to buy a new car… reflecting that banks are back into their main business, for which they were created, which is not other than selling money.

Remember that no long ago, banks insisted on selling their properties –it was a priority within their targets- then they started to sell car and home insurances… and now they are back on track. Banks sell money again!

In these moments funding is really cheap, so borrowing money now is very interesting. For that reason, we have to take advantage to apply for funding to banks, as the interest rates are low and payment terms are long. If we take into consideration the Euribor, it has been in negative since February 2016 and this trend continued during 2017 as we can see in the graph 9, with a -0.190 value in December 2017.

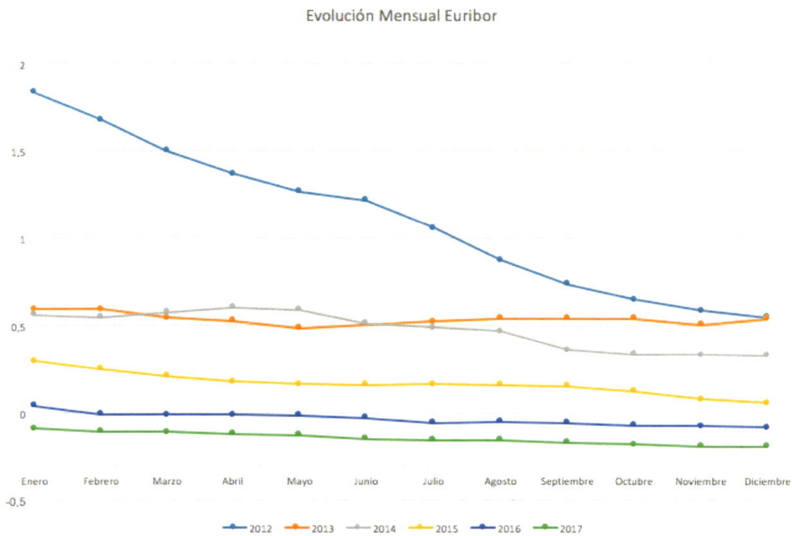

(fig 9)

Mortgage granting increased a 12.4% as a domestic average in September 2017 compared to the prior year. They amounted to 123,649€ on average, which records an increase of 9.64% in the annual rate.

If you are the final purchaser, the average funding that you can get from the Spanish financial entities is the 80% of the purchase value of the property or its appraisal value (the financial entity will use the lowest value), although there are no regulations prohibiting banks to grant mortgages over that 80%.

This bank policy about the funding percentage implies that nowadays the purchaser of a property needs to have saved the 20% of the value of the property plus the expenses generated during the purchase, which, depending on whether it is a new construction or a second-hand property and the autonomous community where the purchase is carried out, may vary between a 10% and a 12%.

It certainly implies that there is a high amount of people who cannot afford to purchase a house, as they cannot save. However, it is a safeguard measure for the real estate and financial market which protects them from crisis as serious as the one suffered from 2007.

In this protective line, the Bank of Spain provided that developers can only get a mortgage in order to purchase land up to the 50% of its value.

Nowadays, the granted fixed-rate mortgages amount to the 38.51% against the variable-rate mortgages which amount to the 61.49%, as we can see in the figure 10.

In fact, some of the financial entities offer fixed interest rates under the 2%, what is very appealing both for domestic clients, who want to avoid unpleasant surprises in the future and be sure about their share to pay for the rest of the loan lifespan, and for international clients, who are more used to this kind of mortgages.

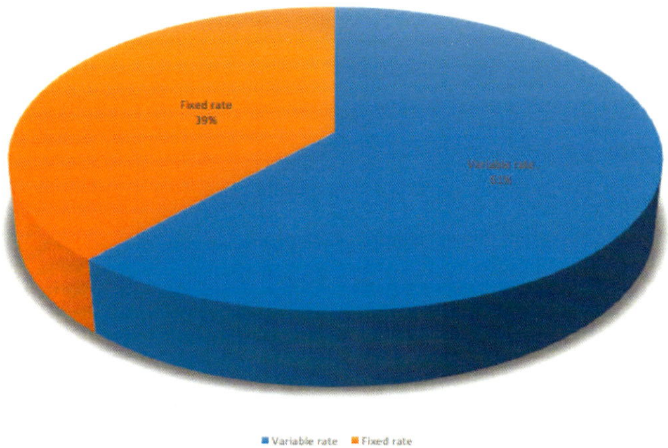

(fig 10)

Nevertheless, the most interesting mortgages for clients are still the variable-rated ones, taking into account that the Euribor was negative in December 2017, with a provisional average of the -0.190. Forecasts tell us that the Euribor is keeping that slight downward trend due to the policies of the European Central Bank, which, undoubtedly, make a variable-rated mortgage more interesting nowadays for mortgage borrowers.

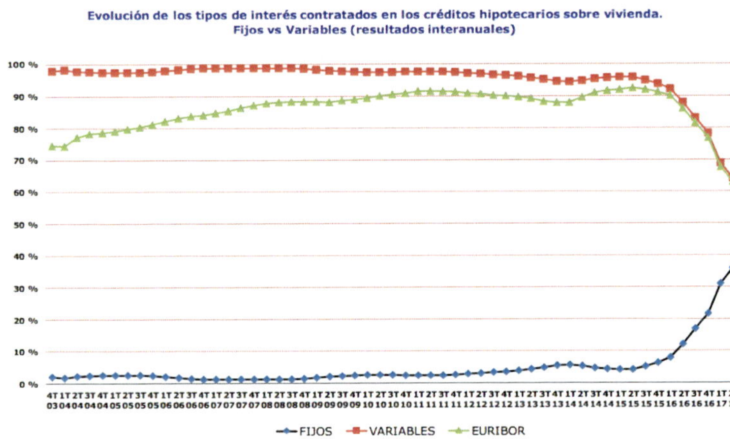

Source: Property Registry (fig 11)

The average interest rate in a mortgage is of the 2.27%, for a term of 23 years and 4 months, and with a monthly payment of 535.87€.

Monthly payments as per Communities:

The Autonomous Communities with higher average monthly mortgage payments are the Community of Madrid (783.33 €), Balearic Islands (705.21 €), Catalonia (645.64 €), Basque Country (578.57 €) and Navarre (480.29 €). On the contrary, the lowest amounts correspond to Extremadura (311.67 €), Murcia (357.74 €), Castilla-La Mancha (392.53 €) and La Rioja (397.95 €). Regarding the percentage of such payment as for the salaries, the hardest affordability levels were reached in the Balearic Islands (40.03%), the Community of Madrid (34.40%), Catalonia (32.09%), Canary Islands (27.41%) and Galicia (26.29%), whereas the most favourable conditions occurred in Extremadura (20.21%), Murcia (20.92%), La Rioja (22.70%), and Asturias (22.95%).

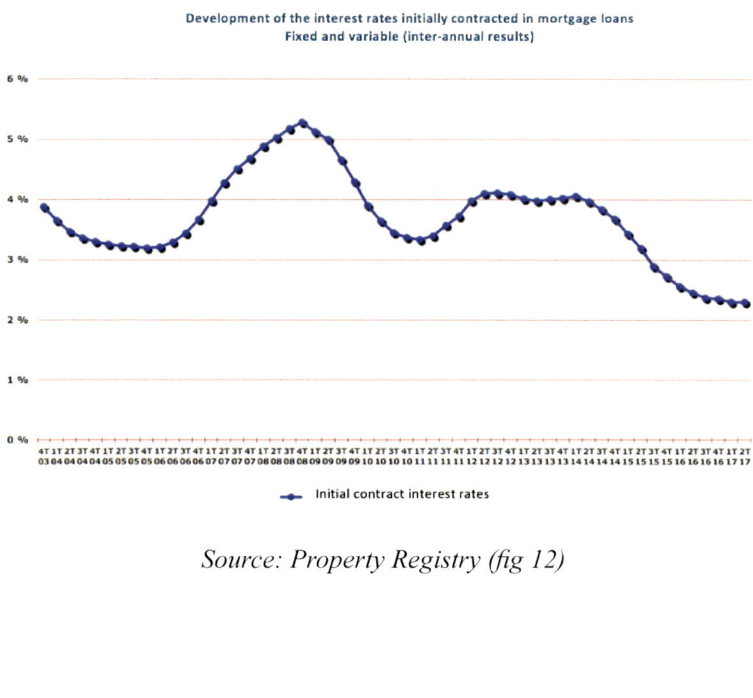

Source: Property Registry (fig 12)

Profitability of property rental:

As the Royal Spanish Academy defines **Profitability,** it is related to a profitable condition and the ability to generate income, which led us to the meaning of generating income: afford or yield profits or earnings yearly.

Another good definition for profitability is: the rate which measures the relation between the earnings or profits obtained and the investment or resources used to get them.

A simple formula to calculate it is:

Profitability = (Earning or profit / Investment) x 100

In the specific case of real estate, apart from this calculation to find out the profitability of an operation, we must add the increase of the price (whether it occurs) of the acquired good.

Year after year, investing on a property becomes more appealing if we focus on the profitability obtained by purchasing a real estate asset to trade with it as a rental afterwards.

In 2017, a house purchased and brought to the rental market got an annual profitability of the 5.7%, and this amount increases year after year as shown in the graph 13.

(fig 13)

To that 5.7%, we must add the 4.4% revaluation that a house gets, according to the Bank of Spain, what generates an annual profitability over the 10% in cities such as Madrid or Alicante.

In Spain, and following a more Europeanist line, we can see it in the graph 14, which compares the stock of rented and owned houses. We must highlight that the highest percentage as for rented houses belongs to

Germany with a 48.1%. Spain, with a 21.8%, is still far from the housing rental levels of Germany, Great Britain, France or Denmark. As to owned houses, in Romania the 96.4% of people own a house.

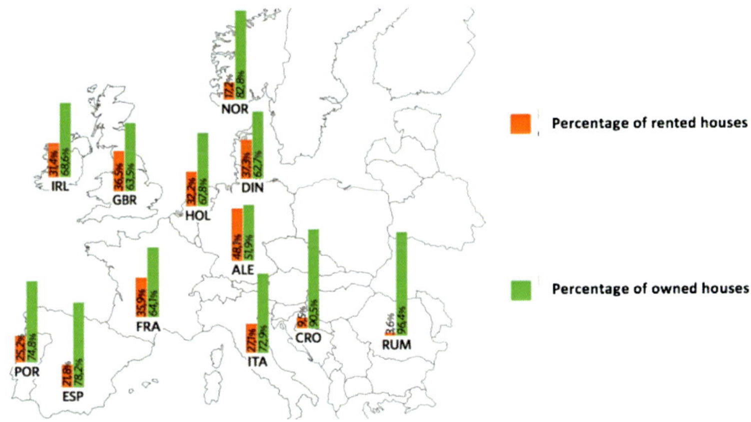

Source: idealista (fig 14)

In Spain, the percentage of people in favour of living in rented houses is increasing compared to the people in favour of living in an owned house –in most of the cases, it is due to the lack of savings or due to the flexibility and freedom which living in a rented house offers you, especially as for your career.

This factor means that purchasing a property from an investor point of view is getting more and more interesting. The portfolio of tenants keeps growing year after year, especially among young people aged from 18 to 24, as the 41% of these people think that they are not becoming the owner of a property in a medium or long term.

The 57% of the Spanish people aged among 25 and 35 cannot save even the 10% of the purchase value of a property, what means that nowadays, and whether funding does not change again in the same direction that years ago when the 100% of the purchase amount was funded and some entities even funded the purchase expenses, these young people are meant to live in rented houses.

Naturally, we cannot forget the importance of holiday rental, especially in the coast, and in big or touristic cities, where an annual increase of the demand and price is noticed thanks to new platforms such as Airbnb and the increase of tourists coming to Spain.

The United Kingdom is still the main market for Spain, with over 2.31 million tourists, followed by French and German visitors.

Everything suggests that in 2017 we had 80 million visitors by the end of the year and, whether this amount does not change, Spain will become the second most visited country in the world, only after France and overtaking the United States.

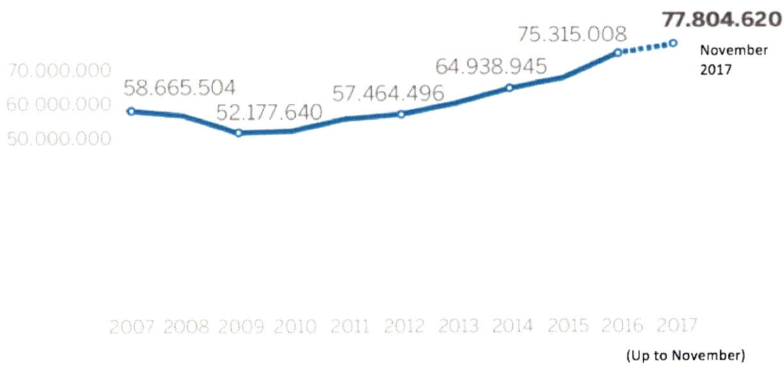

Source: El País fig (15)

I have clients who invested on the purchase of a property in 2015 and nowadays they are getting a gross profitability over the 5% a year. We should add to this percentage the increase of the property price, which sometimes can reach an appraisal over the 20%.

During the years 2014 and 2015, one of the most repeated questions by clients who wanted to buy a house was: Adrián, do you think that prices will continue decreasing or they have already bottomed out? Purchasers still hesitated whether the purchase they wanted to do was the most profitable for them or whether they should wait some more time until prices continue decreasing.

In the cases in which clients decided to rely on my advice and made the decision to purchase a property, they got it right. Finally, time proved I was right and the clients who decided to purchase in those years (mostly properties owned by banks) are obtaining a high profitability nowadays.

Once I read in one of the books by Warren Buffet that he had had several opportunities to make a good deal by selling his family house but for him that house plenty of memories and experiences was not worth to be sold just to get an economic profit.

Actually, this is the big difference: a person who wants to purchase a house to live with his/her family or a person who wants to invest on real estate.

In the case of a property which is an investment, the client does not need to like it. It is just a financial operation. It does not matter whether the living room or the bedrooms of the house are wider or narrower, or whether the kitchen is equipped with the latest technical advances. It is a matter of being aware of and able to estimate very accurately the future sales value of that property and get money by renting it for a period of time.

The purchase of a house to live, a home in the end, is a decision made with your heart. However, when we talk about purchasing a property to invest and try to make money, it is a decision made using your mind, thinking and assessing all the factors (not only the economic ones) which are involved and which will be decisive for the investment.

Why does a foreign client decide to buy in Spain?

There are several factors which make Spain a very interesting country to purchase a property, especially if we talk about an investment or the purchase of a 'holiday home' for foreign people.

-**Weather**: our country has a fantastic weather, especially in the coast, where we have mild temperatures during the whole year, with an average of 320 sunny days a year and scarce rains, what makes it a real paradise for foreign people, especially for those who live in Nordic countries.

-**Gastronomy**: our gastronomy includes a wide range of regional and Mediterranean dishes among which we highlight the Paella, which is a dish known all around the world. In many restaurants, the menus are written in Spanish, English, Russian... and depending on the area, in Dutch, Norwegian... what reflects our superb service to foreign clients. Spanish cuisine is in vogue and nowadays there are two Spanish chefs in the top 10 of the best chefs worldwide and 3 of our restaurants are also in the world's top 10.

-**Beaches**: we have very high-quality beaches and what is more important, they are public. Many people ignore that Spain leads the world's ranking of blue flags with 684 (including beaches with 579 flags, ports with 100 and tourist boats with 5). Greece comes after Spain in this ranking as it was a great competitor, until its last debt crisis, together with Italy on the sale of holiday homes and holidays in the Mediterranean.

-**European reliability:** Spain guarantees to purchasers that it is a democratic country, very respectful with the different cultures coexisting here, as well as it is supported by the European Union. This reliability is also reflected in the bank transfers.

-**Hotel quality**: a first step to attract the attention of these clients is usually their first stay in a hotel. It is true that the reputation of Spanish hotels is much higher than the global average and we all are aware that a 3-star hotel here often corresponds to a 4-star hotel abroad.

-**Health care:** In this area we may have two options. One is the medical recommendation for the patient to move to Spain, especially to the coast, because of the weather that the patient will enjoy, the importance of the sunlight and the good temperatures which may be very significant for a treatment.

The second option is the health tourism which is increasing at a 20% rate every year in Spain, and according to some recent reports, this business will generate a turnover of 1,000 million Euros in 2020. In this case, foreigners usually come from markets such as the European, Arabic and Russian, but also from the Latin American and Chinese markets, which are getting more relevance.

Patients come for reasons such as the quality of healthcare, access to treatments which they do not always have in their countries, the lack of a waiting list, a competitive price, post-surgical convenience and, finally, as I mentioned before, the good weather.

How will future sales be?

We are approaching 2020 and cars still do not fly, but it is true that technology is taking giant steps and in the next years we will see many changes, for instance, in 3 years time, internet users will consume the 80% of its content as a video. Today's figure is still far from that 80%, but the evolution is coming fast.

In the real estate market there have not been dramatic changes up to now in the construction or sales of properties, but there are technologies which are starting to change both processes:

-**Drones**: they have already been used for some years by the developers to offer to the client a real picture of the views from his/her flat – for instance-, it is not infographics or something to be imagined, it is a real image as the drone rises up to the level of the corresponding floor and takes photographs of the views. Time is over for suppositions such as whether a flat in the fourth floor will have sea views or not, as well as having to trust the seller's words about the sea views from a second floor. Now, with the drone, the client can see the reality of what he/she will find in his/her new house in some months.

-**PropTech**: The PropTech industry is based on the users' experience, in the data and their analysis. This industry is gaining market share fast all around the world, and its main business centre is located in New York. This industry aims to bring value to the real estate market by boosting its transformation. Part of this 'new' industry is made up of apps, virtual reality, blockchain… Some of these instruments are going to be analyzed in deep hereinafter.

-**Virtual reality** applied to the real estate market. It definitely sounds good. Which Norwegian wouldn't like to visit his/her future property in Spain from his/her living room in Oslo?

Virtual reality is coming to change the way to sell properties. But we do not just have to focus on foreign clients, let's think of a person aiming to purchase a house in Madrid who can visit all the new developments on construction from the living room of his/her current house. The client's feeling could be really close to reality even when the house has not been built yet, as it is not just a matter of seeing, but also feeling and getting excited. The client could see the common areas, the finishes, the environment or any other interesting detail for him/her. The British real estate platform Rightmove started to include virtual reality trials last year.

Goldman Sachs considers that virtual reality, which seems to be far from now, will be a business exceeding the 2,600 million Dollars in the global real estate market by 2025 (which is so close indeed).

-**Blockchain:** what is it? Blockchain is a technology which is or will be able to change our connection to the digital world. Designed in 2008, Blockchain works as a chronologic database which safely records all the transactions through a peer-to peer shared net. The transaction chain may be publicly verified.

It aims to reduce fraud, turn transactions more secure and speed up the purchase and sale terms. You can digitally check that all the information about a property is lawful as there will be a sales and purchase history. Thus, the process will be more transparent and we will find out who purchased one or another property, the prices, the amount of prior transactions and the property history. The prices of the properties will be allocated by computer as for the sales history and the current situation of the market.

Sweden is the first western country implementing this tool as a trial in the real estate market, making an agreement between the purchaser, the seller, the financial entity and the government. The trial has been positive and they intend to implement it permanently.

- **3D printer:** Time ago I read that in some years luggage will disappear as we will travel with the clothes in our backs and we will have a 3D printer in the hotel's room or the rental apartment (as there is a coffee machine nowadays) to print clothes for the next day. Creating clothes is indeed surprising, but there are already ideas about giant 3D printers that could print a two-storey house in 24 hours, what will allow us to choose structures freely without the restrictions of conventional construction.

-**Crowdlending**: the first leading platform in the real estate market in Spain has been launched recently with the authorization of the National Stock Exchange Commission and the Bank of Spain. This kind of platform mediates among developers and investors, speeding up the bureaucratic processes and simplifying the administrative processes to collect funds quickly in exchange for an interest rate.

Personally, I am not sceptical at all about the advances and the changes which we will soon appreciate thanks to PropTech, FinTech, Crowdlending, Wework, Smart Cities… So, we will see what the close future holds for the real estate market, but I consider that the way to sell and purchase a property will be completely different from today's.

In November, the first auction of a public real estate was carried out on the Internet, what speeded up and made much easier the process. And it is just one more example of how is the market developing.

7 best-kept secrets to know if you are before a good Real Estate Agent

"Honesty is a very expensive gift. Don't expect it from cheap people"

Warren Buffet

-The Real Estate Agent who helps you in the purchase process must be HONEST. It is a non-negotiable quality which your Real Estate Agent must have. He/she must be a reasonable, fair and truthful person.

- Is you agent a QUALIFIED REAL ESTATE AGENT? As Albert Einstein used to say: "We are all very ignorant. What happens is that not all ignore the same things". It is important that your agent is trained in the real estate market and able to lead you during all the purchase process in a reliable manner.

-Professional references. Do you know the career of the agent who is with you during the purchase process? Check the opinions of the clients who already purchased a property with him/her, they are your best certificate. The best assessment of an agent is made by his/her clients, in the same way as you check the recommendations or reviews before booking a travel or buying an item in Amazon.

-Do you know the professional experience of your Real Estate Agent? Is it wide enough to rely on him/her?

-Your agent must be professional and he/she must get involved during the whole purchase process. Additionally, he/she must be polite, empathic and a good listener.

-A good agent replies quickly to a client's questions and concerns.

-It is essential that your agent is good at communicating, in a one-to-one relationship, and at negotiating.

Conclusion:

To sum up, I would like to highlight the following keys about why is it a good moment to purchase or invest on a property in Spain:

Key 1: In 2017, the real estate market had a 5.7% annual profitability, to which we must add the property revaluation

Key 2: Inexpensive mortgages fostered by low interest rates, what means that you will be able to contract a fix-rate mortgage and sleep soundly.

Key 3: The reappearance of developers which put their new properties in the market so that the client can choose between a wider range as well as choose between a second-hand property or a new construction property.

Key 4: The amount of purchase and sale operations has also increased compared to the last years.

And I do not want to finish this book without making **a forecast** for **2018** about the development of the real estate market. I believe the domestic price of properties will increase among a 4% and a 6% in Spain this year, although it is certain that some cities such as Madrid or Alicante will increase over such percentages.

The amount of purchases and sales will increase around a 10% over the sales carried out in 2017, what may also imply an increase in the mortgage granting which will keep inexpensive interest rates.

New developers will turn up as well as very interesting new projects to invest, most of them with modern finishes and straight lines.

Bank's real estate agencies will progress on the sales of their property stock, which should be a small and insignificant stock by 2020.

Finally, as for the technological advances, I believe that we will not appreciate big changes in the property sales in 2018, even though I am sure we will see more videos for real estate marketing. Therefore, we will have to wait until 2019 so virtual or augmented reality becomes a common practice in property sales.

Some ideas or tips to bear in mind before investing:

-Whether it is about real estate, buy at a low price, sell at a high price and do not be greedy.

-Analyze thoroughly and become an expert of the right place to invest. Wherever rich people spend their leisure time is said to be a good place to invest.

-Make your decision asap, if you spend much time thinking about purchasing, you will not do it.

-Think long-term, but act short-term on opportunities.

-Understand your goals within a specific term for each investment.

-Whether you have a good deal, go for it and stop negotiating.

-The most successful projects turn out whenever people working on them pay attention to hundreds of small details which their competitors ignore.

- Always choose quality, try to purchase quality products.

-Access to all the information as far as possible about the property before purchasing it.

-Today's tenant is tomorrow's buyer.

-There are always opportunities.

-The purchase price is crucial to make a good business in the future.

-Consider thoroughly the growing potential of the location.

-Remember that the real estate market is cyclical.

-If you are looking for a house to live, buy listening to your heart instead of your mind. But if you are looking for investment, start thinking.

Sources checked for this book

Spanish National Statistics Institute

Confidencial [newspaper]

Bank of Spain

Expansión [newspaper]

Idealista [Real estate webpage]

El Mundo [newspaper]

El País [newspaper]

Tinsa [An appraisal corporation]

Spanish Ministry of Public Works and Transport

Notary's Association

Spanish Registrars